NATIONAL GEOGRAPHIC

D0602864

My Cat and I

Regina Schirmer

My cat has two eyes.

So do I.

My cat has two ears.

So do I.

My cat has one nose.

So do I.

My cat has one tail.
I don't.